AMAZING ANIMALS
OF THE WORLD 2

Volume 8

Reedbuck, Mountain — Snake, Tentacled

GROLIER

First published 2005 by Grolier, an imprint of Scholastic Library Publishing

For information address the publisher: Grolier, Scholastic Library Publishing
90 Old Sherman Turnpike
Danbury, CT 06816

Set ISBN: 0-7172-6112-3; Volume ISBN: 0-7172-6120-4

Printed and bound in the U.S.A.

Library of Congress Cataloging-in-Publications Data:
Amazing animals of the world 2.
p.cm.
Includes indexes.
Contents: v. 1. Adder—Buffalo, Water -- v. 2. Bunting, Corn—Cricket, Bush -- v. 3. Cricket, European Mole—Frog, Agile -- v. 4. Frog, Burrowing Tree—Guenon, Moustached -- v. 5. Gull, Great Black-backed—Loach, Stone -- v. 6. Locust, Migratory—Newt, Crested -- v. 7. Nuthatch, Eurasian—Razor, Pod -- v. 8. Reedbuck, Mountain—Snake, Tentacled -- v. 9. Snakefly—Toad, Surinam -- v. 10. Tortoise, Gopher—Zebu.
ISBN 0-7172-6112-3 (set : alk. paper) -- ISBN 0-7172-6113-1 (v. 1 : alk. paper) -- ISBN 0-7172-6114-X (v. 2 : alk. paper) -- ISBN 0-7172-6115-8 (v. 3 : alk. paper) -- ISBN 0-7172-6116-6 (v. 4 : alk. paper) -- ISBN 0-7172-6117-4 (v. 5 : alk. paper) -- ISBN 0-7172-6118-2 (v. 6 : alk. paper) -- ISBN 0-7172-6119-0 (v. 7 : alk. paper) -- ISBN 0-7172-6120-4 (v. 8 : alk. paper) -- ISBN 0-7172-6121-2 (v. 9 : alk. paper) -- ISBN 0-7172-6122-0 (v. 10 : alk.paper)
1. Animals--Juvenile literature. I. Title: Amazing animals of the world two. II. Grolier (Firm)
QL49.A455 2005
590--dc22
2005040351

About This Set

Amazing Animals of the World 2 brings you pictures of 400 fascinating creatures and important information about how and where they live.

Each page shows just one species—individual type—of animal. They all fall into seven main categories or groups of animals (classes and phylums scientifically) that appear on each page as an icon or picture—amphibians, arthropods, birds, fish, mammals, other invertebrates, and reptiles. Short explanations of what these group names mean, and other terms used commonly in the set, appear on page 4 in the Glossary.

Scientists use all kinds of groupings to help them sort out the thousands of types of animals that exist today and once wandered here (extinct species). Kingdoms, classes, phylums, genus, and species are among the key words here that are also explained in the Glossary (page 4).

Where animals live is important to know as well. Each of the species in this set lives in a particular place in the world, which you can see outlined on the map on each page. And in those locales the animals tend to favor a particular habitat—an environment the animal finds suitable for life, with food, shelter, and safety from predators that might eat it. There they also find ways to coexist with other animals in the area that might eat somewhat different food, use different homes, and so on. Each of the main habitats is named on the page and given an icon/picture to help you envision it. The habitat names are further defined in the Glossary on page 4.

As well as being part of groups like species, animals fall into other categories that help us understand their lives or behavior. You will find these categories in the Glossary on page 4, where you will learn about carnivores, herbivores, and other types of animals.

And there is more information you might want about an animal—its size, diet, where it lives, and how it carries on its species—the way it creates its young. All these facts and more appear in the data boxes at the top of each page.

Finally, you should know that the set is arranged alphabetically by the most common name of the species. That puts most beetles, say, together in a group so you can compare them easily.

But some animals' names are not so common, and they don't appear near others like them. For instance, the chamois is a kind of goat or antelope. To find animals that are similar—or to locate any species—look in the index at the end of each book in the set (pages 45-48). It lists all animals by their various names (you will find the giant South American river turtle under turtle, giant South American river, and also under its other name—arrau). And you will find all birds, fish, and so on gathered under their broader groupings.

Similarly, smaller like groups appear in the set index as well—butterflies include swallowtails and blues, for example.

Table of Contents
Volume 8

Glossary

Amphibians—species usually born from eggs in water or wet places, which change (metamorphose) into a land animal. Frogs and salamanders are typical. They breathe through their skin mainly and have no scales.

Arctic and Antarctic—icy, cold, dry areas at the ends of the globe that lack trees but see small plants grown in thawed areas (tundra). Penguins and seals are common inhabitants.

Arthropods—animals with segmented bodies, hard outer skin, and jointed legs, such as spiders and crabs.

Birds—born from eggs, these creatures have wings and often can fly. Eagles, pigeons, and penguins are all birds, though penguins can't fly through the air.

Carnivores—they are animals that eat other animals. Many species do eat each other sometimes, and a few eat dead animals. Lions kill their prey and eat it, while vultures clean up dead bodies of animals.

Cities, Towns, and Farms—places where people live and have built or used the land and share it with many species. Sometimes these animals live in human homes or just nearby.

Class—part or division of a phylum.

Deserts—dry, often warm areas where animals often are more active on cooler nights or near water sources. Owls, scorpions, and jack rabbits are common in American deserts.

Endangered—some animals in this set are marked as endangered because it is possible they will become extinct soon.

Extinct—these species have died out altogether for whatever reason.

Family—part of an order.

Fish—water animals (aquatic) that typically are born from eggs and breathe through gills. Trout and eels are fish, though whales and dolphins are not (they are mammals).

Forests and Mountains—places where evergreen (coniferous) and leaf-shedding (deciduous) trees are common, or that rise in elevation to make cool, separate habitats. **Rainforests are different (see below).**

Fresh Water—lakes, rivers, and the like carry fresh water (unlike Oceans and Shores, where the water is salty). Fish and birds abound, as do insects, frogs, and mammals.

Genus—part of a family.

Grasslands—habitats with few trees and light rainfall. Grasslands often lie between forests and deserts, and they are home to birds, coyotes, antelope, and snakes, as well as many other kinds of animals.

Herbivores—these animals eat mainly plants. Typical are hoofed animals (ungulates) that are common on grasslands, such as antelope or deer. Domestic (nonwild) ones are cows and horses.

Hibernators—species that live in harsh areas with very cold winters slow down their functions then and sort of sleep through the hard times.

Kingdom—the largest division of species. Commonly there are understood to be five kingdoms: animals, plants, fungi, protists, and monerans.

Mammals—these creatures usually bear live young and feed them on milk from the mother. A few lay eggs (monotremes like the platypus) or nurse young in a pouch (marsupials like opossums and kangaroos).

Migrators—some species spend different seasons in different places, moving to where more food, warmth, or safety can be found. Birds often do this, sometimes over long distances, but others types of animals also move seasonally, including fish and mammals.

Oceans and Shores—seawater is salty, often deep, and huge. In it live many fish, invertebrates, and even some mammals, such as whales. On the shore birds and other creatures often gather.

Order—part of a class.

Other Invertebrates—animals that lack backbones or internal skeletons. Many, such as insects and shrimp, have hard outer coverings. Clams and worms are also invertebrates.

Phylum—part of a kingdom.

Rainforests—here huge trees grow among many other plants helped by the warm, wet environment. Thousands of species of animals also live in these rich habitats.

Reptiles—these species have scales, lungs to breathe, and lay eggs or give birth to live young. Dinosaurs are thought to have been reptiles, while today the class includes turtles, snakes, lizards, and crocodiles.

Scientific name—the genus and species name of a creature in Latin. For instance, Canis lupus is the wolf. Scientific names avoid the confusion possible with common names in any one language or across languages.

Species—a group of the same type of living thing. Part of an order.

Subspecies—a variant but quite similar part of a species.

Territorial—many animals mark out and defend a patch of ground as their home area. Birds and mammals may call quite small or quite large spots their territories.

Vertebrates—animals with backbones and skeletons under their skins

Mountain Reedbuck
Redunca fulvorufula

Length of the Body: 3½ to 4 feet

Length of the Tail: 6¾ to 10½ inches

Diet: grasses, herbs, and leaves

Number of Young: 1; rarely 2

Home: Africa

Weight: 44 to 66 pounds

Order: Even-toed hoofed mammals

Family: Bovines

 Forests and Mountains

Mammals

© INGRID VAN DEN BERG / ANIMALS ANIMALS / EARTH SCENES

Africa is home to three species of reedbuck: the common reedbuck, the Bohor reedbuck, and the mountain reedbuck. All are sturdy antelope named for their habit of living in reed beds near fresh water. Reedbuck are more solitary than other types of antelope, but the mountain species differs from its two cousins in several ways.

As its name suggests, the mountain reedbuck is found at high elevations, usually on hilly and rocky terrain. There are few lakes and reed beds in its habitat, so the reedbuck has learned to survive farther from water than its relatives. This creature is also more social than the others. While common and Bohor reedbuck live alone for much of

the year, mountain reedbuck gather in large troops of up to 40 animals. The troop usually includes several females, their offspring, and one or two males.

Mountain reedbuck are similar to the other reedbuck in appearance, although they are smaller and lighter in weight. All reedbuck have a naked patch of dark skin—about the size of a nickel—in front of each ear. This skin patch produces a scent that the reedbuck wafts into the air by waggling its ears. The animals use the scent to warn away competitors and to attract mates. In South Africa, mountain reedbuck give birth from November to March. The young mature in about 1½ years and live to be at least 12 years old.

Reedfish
Calamoichthys calabaricus

Diet: insects, worms, crustaceans, and small fish
Method of Reproduction: egg layer

Home: West Africa
Length: up to 35½ inches
Order: Bichirs and reedfishes
Family: Reedfishes

 Fresh Water

 Fish

© HANS REINHARD / BRUCE COLEMAN INC.

The beautiful olive-green reedfish is sometimes called a "living fossil," because it is from a family of fish that became all but extinct before the first humans had been born. The reedfish and its living relatives, the bichirs, have changed little in the 65 million years they have been on earth. They share with their extinct relatives a simple skull structure and a long, almost finless body. Actually, the reedfish has many tiny "finlets" barely visible along the top side of the fish's primitive, snakelike body.

The young reedfish, or larvae, are born with gills and breathe as most modern fish do—by extracting oxygen from the water in which they swim. In contrast, adult reedfish swim to the surface of the water and gulp down air from the atmosphere. This allows the reedfish to live in very muddy streams that would choke water-breathing fish. When a reedfish breathes air, it inhales into a primitive lung called a swim bladder. Many modern fish have swim bladders as well. But they take air into their swim bladders only to help them float—not to get oxygen.

As its name implies, the slender reedfish lives among reeds and other thickly growing plants. It makes its home in the slow-flowing streams and still waters of West Africa. At night the reedfish slithers slowly along the stream bottom, hunting for insects, worms, small fish, and crustaceans. It rests during the day, well hidden among the reeds.

Reindeer (Caribou)
Rangifer tarandus

Length: 4½ to 8½ feet
Weight: 132 to 700 pounds
Number of Young: usually 1
Home: Canada, northern Eurasia, and northwestern United States

Diet: lichen, herbs, fungi, leaves, and buds
Order: Even-toed hoofed mammals
Family: Deer

  Grasslands

 Mammals

© DARRELL GULIN / CORBIS

Of all the world's deer, caribou do the most running. They can run faster and farther than any other species. Caribou need their speed and endurance to escape from their enemies. Should a caribou get a running start across the flat Arctic tundra, no natural predator can catch it! Still, hunters and wolves kill many of these creatures. In addition, young caribou are often captured by grizzly bears, lynx, wolverines, and golden eagles. Even insects cause caribou to flee. In summer, biting blackflies and mosquitoes torture these large deer. To escape the maddening insects, caribou run, dive into water, roll in snow, and stand in strong winds.

Biologists now recognize the caribou of North America and the reindeer of Europe and Asia as one and the same species. Specially adapted for year-round cold, caribou are at home on the Arctic tundra and in snowy northern forests. The caribou's milk is the richest of any hoofed animal. The calves need this high-energy fuel, because they grow quickly in strength and size. A newborn can stand after just 30 minutes and run within an hour and a half.

The male caribou has the heaviest antlers of any deer, and only among the caribou do females bear antlers as well. The reindeer of Europe is the only deer in the world to be truly domesticated. For hundreds of years, Scandinavians have raised reindeer for their milk and meat. Other reindeer are trained to pull sleds...even Santa's, some say.

Roach
Rutilus rutilus

Length: 6 to 18 inches
Diet: crustaceans, mollusks, plants, and algae
Method of Reproduction: egg layer

Weight: 1 to 3 pounds
Home: Europe and Asia
Order: Carps and their relatives
Family: Carps

 Fresh Water

Fish

© TOM MCHUGH / PHOTO RESEARCHERS

Mention an animal named "roach," and most people think of the disgusting creature that lurks in kitchens and scatters when the lights are turned on. However, that creepy, crawly roach is formally called a cockroach. By contrast, the animal correctly called roach is a beautifully colored fish that lives in Europe and Asia. The roach has an olive or gray-green back with a silvery shine, yellowish-silver sides, and reddish fins.

Roaches are most common in weedy lakes and slow-flowing rivers. They live in groups called schools or shoals. In warm weather, schools stay in shallow areas; they move to deeper waters for the winter.

Roaches reproduce in April and May. Schools that live in salty water migrate upstream to reproduce in fresh water. Males usually arrive at the spawning site a few days before the females. A female roach may lay as many as 150,000 transparent yellowish eggs among aquatic plants. At the same time, the males release sperm. How many of the eggs are fertilized is simply a matter of chance.

Young roaches have huge appetites for small crustaceans, insect larvae, and plant matter. Adult roaches eat larger crustaceans, mollusks, and plants. In turn, roaches are eaten by such predators as herons, otters, pike, and perch. In many parts of Europe and Asia, roaches are an important human food.

Common Roller
Coracias garrulus

Length: about 12 inches
Weight: about 5 ounces
Number of Eggs: 4 to 6
Home: *Summer:* Europe, Asia, and northern Africa
Winter: eastern Africa

Diet: insects, small lizards, frogs, small birds, and fruits
Order: Kingfishers and their relatives
Family: Rollers

 Cities, Towns, and Farms

 Birds

Summer
Winter

© ERIC AND DAVID HOSKING / CORBIS

At first glance the common roller looks like a large bluebird or blue jay, but with even handsomer plumage: bright chestnut on the back with wings that are a vivid blue, just a shade darker than its pale blue breast and head. Its tail is green, with brown feathers at the center. And unlike many bird species, both male and female common rollers are colorful.

The common roller has a long, strong beak with a sharp, downward-curving tip. The beak is designed for snatching and holding small prey. From its typical perching place on bare branches and overhead wires, the roller watches for flying insects, which it catches in midair. Rollers also dive after small animals such as lizards and frogs, and even attack smaller birds. They are fearsome predators but are quite friendly among themselves. They frequently join in large, chattering flocks.

Rollers are named for the acrobatic flight of the courting male. In spring, he tries to impress his mate with a somersaulting dive from high in the sky. After mating, the pair makes a nest in a tree hole or in the soil. After the female lays her eggs, the parents take turns warming them for about 18 days. They both care for the chicks.

Rollers spend the spring and summer in Europe, northern Africa, and southwestern Asia. In fall, they fly to warmer winter homes in eastern and southern Africa.

9

Lilac-breasted Roller
Coracias caudata

Length: about 14½ inches
Weight: 3 to 4 ounces
Number of Eggs: 2 or 3
Home: eastern and southern Africa

Diet: lizards and insects
Order: Kingfishers and their relatives
Family: Rollers

 Rainforests

 Birds

© JOE MCDONALD / CORBIS

ew people can forget the sight of a lilac-breasted roller tumbling and somersaulting through the air. The male roller performs his aerial acrobatics in September, the start of breeding season. After soaring high into the air, he tumbles downward with what seems to be reckless abandon. Just before crashing, he rights himself and soars upward again.

Once their flamboyant courtship is over, mated rollers become quite shy. The pair retreat to a secluded area to build their nest, typically in a hole in a dead tree. They sometimes scratch a nest in the side of a tall anthill, which provides great quantities of food as well as shelter.

In addition to eating ants, the agile roller catches small lizards. These intelligent birds often follow grass fires and catch lizards that flee from the flames. As they hunt, lilac-breasted rollers call loudly with a hoarse, screeching cry.

Males and females are equally colorful. The light purple of their breast feathers blends with the greenish-blue feathers on their belly and legs. Their rump and outer wings are violet, while the base of their wing feathers is a pale green-blue. In southern and eastern Africa, lilac-breasted rollers are often seen singly or in pairs, perched on telephone wires or on the tops of tall thorn trees and palms.

Black Ruby
Barbus nigrofasciatus

Length: 2½ inches
Diet: debris, algae, mollusks, insects, and arthropods
Method of Reproduction: egg layer

Home: Sri Lanka
Order: Carps and carplike fishes
Family: Barb fishes

Fresh Water

Fish

© JANE BURTON / BRUCE COLEMAN INC.

The black ruby earns its name during the breeding season. During most of the year, this fish wears a dull "prison uniform" of black stripes on a dirty-gray background. But when it's ready to mate, the male black ruby changes color to a brilliant red. Its dark stripes turn a velvety green highlighted by glittering green spots. To top off the show, the fish's dorsal fin (located on its back) is purple. After spawning, the black ruby regains its modest coloration.

The black ruby's colorful display makes it a popular aquarium fish. It is not shy about mating in captivity and will produce lots of offspring. Experts suggest placing black rubies in a tank near an eastern-facing window. These fish prefer to spawn in the early-morning sunshine. It also helps to provide some floating plants for shelter. In the wild the black ruby can be found in the meandering streams of Sri Lanka. It prefers to live in the sheltering shade of riverbank trees. There it hides among sunken branches and between fronds of underwater vegetation.

The black ruby belongs to a large group, or family, of fish called "barb fishes." Even its scientific name, *Barbus*, comes from the barbels, or whiskers, that this type of fish uses to taste its food before eating. However, nature has given the black ruby a close shave. Although its ancestors probably wore whiskers, the black ruby is a barb fish without the barbs.

Rudd
Scardinius erythrophthalmus

Length: up to 19 inches
Method of Reproduction: egg layer
Home: native to Europe and western Asia; introduced elsewhere

Diet: crustaceans, insect larvae, and aquatic plants
Order: Carps and their relatives
Family: Carps

 Fresh Water

 Fish

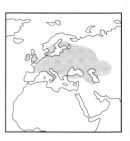

© WIL MEINDERTS / FOTO NATURA / MINDEN PICTURES

The rudd sports colors straight out of a crayon box. This bright fish has a brownish-green back, bright yellow sides, and red fins. Even its red-spotted yellow eyes attract attention.

The rudd lives in the quiet waters of ponds, slow-moving rivers, and marshes—anywhere with an abundance of heavy plant growth. There it hides among the aquatic plants, searching for mosquitoes and other insects. Its mouth is set at an angle—very useful for capturing prey at the water's surface. Although the rudd does not have teeth in its mouth, it has three rows of teeth on the pharyngeal bone near its gills. The teeth grind insects, plant matter, and other food.

The rudd reproduces in spring. Males and females release their sperm and eggs into the water. The eggs are fertilized and stick to aquatic plants before hatching in 3 to 10 days. The baby fish, called fry, are born with tiny yolk sacs that contain food. The young fish hang onto their "home plant" until their bodies have absorbed the nourishing yolk.

The rudd is a native of Eurasia, but people have introduced the fish to the eastern United States and elsewhere. Although not commercially important, the rudd is caught by sport fishermen using hooked fishing lines. If you ever catch one, you'll never forget its striking colors!

Common Dusky Salamander
Desmognathus fuscus

Length: 2½ to 5½ inches
Diet: insect larvae, pill bugs, and worms
Home: eastern United States and Canada

Number of Eggs: 12 to 36
Order: Salamanders and newts
Family: Lungless salamanders

  Fresh Water

Amphibians

© JACK DERMID / BRUCE COLEMAN INC.

This amphibian is the most familiar of the dusky salamanders, which are named for their brown coloration and dark blotches. The common dusky is distinguished from similar species by the triangular shape of its tail, the sides of which come to a pointed ridge at the top.

Scientists have identified two subspecies of dusky salamander. The northern dusky, *D. fuscus fuscus*, is shown in the photo. It is completely brown as an adult, but is covered with yellow spots when young. Northern duskies are found in cold springs and woodland streams. To the south lives the spotted dusky, *D. fuscus conanti*. It does not lose its colorful spots as it ages. Spotted duskies are most common in the muddy areas near mountain streams and on valley floodplains. Common duskies often share their habitats with other salamander species. The dusky avoids competition by staying closer to the surface of a spring or stream than do most salamanders.

Duskies breed throughout the summer and into September. After mating, the female lays a round clump of eggs on a stream bank. Six to 13 weeks later, the gill-breathing hatchlings tumble into the water. It takes three to four years for the hatchlings to mature into adults. Like other lungless salamanders, adult duskies absorb oxygen directly through their skin.

Fire Salamander
Salamandra salamandra

Length: 6 to 12 inches
Length at Birth: ½ to ¾ inch
Diet: insects and earthworms
Number of Young: 15 to 25

Home: Europe, Africa, and Asia
Order: Tailed amphibians
Family: Salamanders

 Forests and Mountains

 Amphibians

© DAVID A. NORTHCOTT / CORBIS

The fire salamander is the largest, most colorful, and best-known salamander in Europe. To look at it, you might think its name comes from its brilliant-yellow spots. They look like flames against the animal's smooth black body. But there is a more mysterious story behind the fire salamander's name. Hundreds of years ago, villagers believed that this animal could live in fire unharmed. Even today, in parts of Europe, the red-hot poker that people keep in a fire is called a "salamander."

In truth, all salamanders like to stay moist and cool. However, this species doesn't spend much time in water. Only the female adult salamander enters the water, and then only halfway. She backs in with her hindquarters to deposit her larva babies. She may lay them in a pond, a wet ditch, or just the water collected in a bicycle track. Salamander larvae look like miniature versions of their parents, except that they have long, feathery gills. They spend about three months in the water, eating tiny insects. During this time, they grow lungs and lose their gills. Then they're ready to leave the water and live on the forest floor.

The skin of the fire salamander is coated with a horrible-tasting poison, strong enough to kill small lizards and snakes. The bad taste also discourages larger predators, who often spit out the distasteful salamander and remember its markings so as not to make the mistake again!

Wood Sandpiper
Tringa glareola

Length: 7¾ to 8 inches
Weight: 2 to 3 ounces
Diet: insects and invertebrates
Number of Eggs: usually 4
Home: *Summer:* Eurasia and Alaska

Winter: northern Africa and southern Asia
Order: Waders and gull-like birds
Family: Sandpipers and their relatives

 Fresh Water

 Birds

Summer ☐ Winter ☐

© TONY HAMBLIN / FRANK LANE PICTURE AGENCY / CORBIS

While most sandpipers build their nests on the beach among the grasses and reeds, the delicate wood sandpiper often nests in the trees. Unable to build its own nest, it takes over an abandoned one from a thrush or shrike. Wood sandpipers also nest on the ground, usually in a soft, mossy depression near the edge of a pond. The bird's eggs are a well-camouflaged light green (to match the moss) with reddish-brown specks. Both parents warm the eggs in shifts. About three weeks after they are laid, the eggs hatch. The tiny chicks chase behind their parents for at least a month, at which time they learn to fly.

Like most northern sandpipers, this species eats mainly insects, worms, and spiders, which it finds along the shores of ponds, lakes, and Arctic seas. Wood sandpipers occasionally jump straight up from the ground, snatching flying insects. To find a special treat—such as a fish or a frog—the bird will swish its long beak through the water. In this way, it can catch prey in water that is too muddy to see through.

Wood sandpipers are always making noise. When flying, they sing a melodious "tleea-tleea-tleea." On the ground, they warble a lilting, two-note phrase—"tlui"—with the second note a little higher in pitch. When danger approaches, the wood sandpiper chatters harshly. "Chiff-chiff-chiff!" it cries to warn its neighbors.

Giant African Scorpion
Pandinus imperator

Length: 7 to 8 inches
Weight: about 2 ounces
Diet: insects, spiders, and
    other small animals

Number of Young: about 32
Home: West Africa
Order: Scorpions
Family: Scorpionid scorpions

 Deserts

 Arthropods

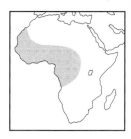

© MATT MEADOWS / PETER ARNOLD, INC.

People are afraid of the scorpion—and for good reason! The insect has a poisonous stinger on the end of its tail. In Africa, people are especially afraid of the giant African scorpion, which is among the world's largest. This creature can easily kill and eat a full-grown mouse, and will also use its stinger to defend itself against a person.

Most arthropods have more babies than you could easily count, and they don't spend much time caring for any of them. In contrast, the giant African scorpion has a rather small number of babies, and it invests a great deal of time in each one. To begin with, a female is pregnant for seven months. That is very long for an arthropod. Then,

when the young are born, they climb onto their mother's back. The mother feeds them and protects them from predators. After 10 to 13 days, the young scorpions either set off on their own or remain with their mother. Those that choose to stay share the duty of gathering food.

It takes from three to seven years for a giant African scorpion to grow to adulthood, depending on how much it has to eat. During this time the scorpion changes its hunting habits. Young, small scorpions sting their prey before eating it. But the older and stronger ones just grab their prey with their forelegs and save their stinger for fighting their own predators.

16

Australian Sea Lion
Neophoca cinerea

Length: 10 feet (male); 5 feet (female)
Weight: 660 pounds (male); 220 pounds (female)
Diet: fish, squid, and crabs
Number of Young: 1

Home: southern coast of Australia
Order: Carnivores
Family: Sea lions and fur seals
Suborder: Seals

 Oceans and Shores

 Mammals

© RALPH A. CLEVENGER / CORBIS

Australian sea lions are known for their aggressiveness. The large male, or bull, who rules the harem, can be quite brutal to his "wives" and offspring. He herds the females along his stretch of beach with loud barks and nasty bites. So fierce are his attacks that many young sea lions die from the wounds. In contrast, the females and young are often quite friendly with one another.

The silver-gray female is less than half the size of the muscular, thick-necked bull. His fur is a dark chocolate brown, and the hair on his neck is slightly longer than hers. In contrast to all other sea lions, the Australian species gives birth over a very long period. The pups may arrive anywhere between October and January.

When it is hungry, the Australian sea lion dives from the rocky shore into the ocean and swims quite far out to sea. There it hunts for fish and squid. The sea lion is sometimes killed by the shark, its only enemy.

To the south lives the Australian sea lion's relative, the New Zealand sea lion. Although the two species look very similar, their personalities are quite different. The gentler bulls of the New Zealand species allow their harems to roam freely along the sandy beaches where they live. Although not endangered, both are protected from hunters because their populations are small.

Baikal Seal
Phoca siberica

Length of the Body: 3¾ to 4½ feet
Weight: 170 to 200 pounds
Diet: fish
Number of Young: 1

Home: Lake Baikal, Russia
Order: Carnivores
Family: Earless seals
Suborder: Pinnipeds

Fresh Water

Mammals

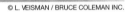
© L. VEISMAN / BRUCE COLEMAN INC.

The Baikal seal lives only in the cold, fresh water of Russia's Lake Baikal. Scientists believe that this species migrated to the lake in prehistoric times, probably from the salty seas surrounding the North Pole. Its close cousins—the ringed seal and the Caspian seal—still live in the icy Arctic waters.

This large, thickly furred seal is grayish-brown on the back and silvery on the belly. Newborns are pure white for the first three to four weeks. Like many furred seals, this species was hunted mercilessly for hundreds of years. During this time, its population plummeted. Russia now limits the number of seals that can be taken each year. The restriction has resulted in the recovery of the seal's population to as many as 50,000.

These seals spend the winter on ice floes in the northern half of their long lake. In summer the seals travel to the lake's southern portions. There they spend more time along the shore than in the water. In mid-March, each pregnant female gives birth to a single white pup. Baikal seals nurse their young for up to 10 weeks, longer than the nursing period of most seals.

Young females mate when they are two to five years old. Males mate at about four years of age. The oldest, largest males often have several mates.

South American Fur Seal
Arctocephalus australis

Length: 4½ to 6 feet
Weight: 110 to 350 pounds
Diet: fish, squid, crabs, mussels, and snails
Number of Young: 1

Home: coastal waters off South America
Order: Carnivores
Family: Sea lions and fur seals
Suborder: Seals

 Oceans and Shores

 Mammals

© FRANCISCO ERIZE / BRUCE COLEMAN INC.

South American fur seals give birth in November and December on rocky South American beaches. The shore where the pups are born is ruled by a single large bull, who chases other adult males away. He mates with the females in his territory shortly after they give birth. But unlike most seal species, these fur seal bulls do not harass or bite their mates and young. The females can come and go as they please.

The first time she leaves her pup, the mother fur seal returns to nurse it the same day. Gradually she increases the length of her hunting trips, until her pup can manage on its own for a full week. During their time alone, fur seal pups amuse themselves by chasing each other over rocks and catching small beach crabs. When the young get bigger and hungrier, the mothers bring them fish. By the end of January, the pups are ready to follow their mother into the sea to hunt.

The ocean can be a dangerous place for fur seals. The seal's natural enemies include sharks and killer whales. In years past, however, South American fur seals suffered worse harm from unnatural predators: humans with spears and guns. Fur seals are valued for their fur, which grows especially long and thick on the male's neck and shoulders. The good news is that most South American countries have now made fur seal hunting illegal.

Sexton (Burying Beetle)
Nicrophorus sp.

Diet: dead animals and plant material
Method of Reproduction: egg layer

Home: worldwide
Length: ¾ to 1¼ inches
Order: Beetles
Family: Carrion beetles

Forests and Mountains

Arthropods

© GARY MESZAROS / PHOTO RESEARCHERS

A sexton, or burying beetle, is recognized by the bright orange-on-black markings on its wing covers. The markings resemble the colors in the robes once worn by church officials called sextons. The beetle's name could also refer to its habit of burying corpses, because church sextons often tended their congregation's cemeteries.

A sexton beetle's body is long, flat, and soft to the touch. This creature is usually the largest of the many insects gathered around the body of a dead animal. In addition to feeding on carcasses, sexton beetles eat dead plants. By doing so, they help recycle a forest's important natural resources.

It is the female sexton beetle that has the interesting habit of burying the bodies of small creatures such as mice, frogs, and snakes. She must work fast, however, before other scavengers eat the dead animal. So she digs furiously beneath the carcass and in this way lowers it into the ground. Sometimes beetles work together to bury a small animal. Before the sextons cover the body with dirt, the females deposit their eggs on the decaying flesh. As a result, when the eggs hatch, the larvae have plenty to eat. According to some accounts, sexton larvae don't feed directly on the carcass, but rather on the numerous fly maggots that develop within it.

Imperial Shag
Phalacrocorax atriceps

Length: about 29 inches
Wingspan: about 49 inches
Weight: about 4⅓ pounds
Diet: fish

Number of Eggs: 2 to 4
Home: southern oceans
Order: Pelicans and gannets
Family: Cormorants and shags

Oceans and Shores

Birds

© JOHN SHAW / BRUCE COLEMAN INC.

The name "imperial shag" was coined in 1978 by scientists who discovered two types of cormorant, previously considered separate species, interbreeding along the southern coast of South America. The scientists combined the two species—the blue-eyed and king cormorants—into one and named it the imperial shag.

The imperial shag is a medium-sized bird designed for life in the water. It has a long, sleek body, elongated neck, and a strong, hooked bill perfectly suited for catching fish. Short, strong legs and large, webbed feet enable the imperial shag to swim with skill and ease. This species hunts in all the oceans of the Southern Hemisphere. While most of its cormorant cousins stay close to shore, the shag often ventures across the open sea.

The darkly colored imperial shag wears a "tuxedo jacket" of blue-black feathers on its back and a snowy-white "bib and shirt" across its neck and underparts. This species is best recognized by striking pink legs and feet and distinctive facial markings—its brown eyes are circled with a ring of bright blue.

During breeding season, adults develop bright patches of orange skin on their face and a wispy crest of head feathers. They nest on bare rocks just a few feet above the high-tide line. There the female lays her pale greenish-blue eggs.

European Angel Shark
Squatina squatina

Length: up to 8 feet
Weight: up to 165 pounds
Diet: small bottom-dwelling fish, mollusks, and crustaceans

Number of Young: 10 to 25
Home: Mediterranean Sea and northeast Atlantic Ocean
Order: Sharks
Family: Angel sharks

 Oceans and Shores

 Fish

© HENRY AUSLOOS / BIOS / PETER ARNOLD, INC.

Despite its name, the European angel shark is no angel. Although not a "man-eater" like some of its more notorious cousins, the European angel shark won't hesitate to use its rough skin and sharp, pointed teeth to severely injure people who mishandle or taunt it. The angel shark derives its name not from its personality but from its fins, which look like the wings of an angel. This creature's other common name—monkfish—refers to the fact that the shark's body looks like that of a monk wearing a robe.

The European angel shark looks like a cross between a shark and a ray. Like rays, it has a flat body and winglike pectoral fins. Its mouth is at the front of the head, whereas most sharks have the mouth on the underside of the head. The angel shark's pectoral fins are loose, while those of a ray are attached to the head. But like all sharks, the angel shark swims by moving its body and tail.

European angel sharks live on the ocean floor. In summer, they move to shallow coastal waters, returning to the deep ocean in winter. There they give birth to their young, well-developed, 8-inch-long "minisharks." Angel sharks feed mainly on bottom-dwelling fish such as soles, plaice, and rays. People living in Mediterranean countries catch angel sharks for their tasty meat.

Great Hammerhead Shark
Sphyrna mokarran

Length: up to 16 feet
Weight: up to 1,000 pounds or more
Diet: stingrays and other fish
Number of Young: 20 to 40

Home: tropical and temperate regions of the Atlantic, Pacific, and Indian oceans
Order: Sharks with two fins
Family: Hammerhead sharks

 Oceans and Shores

 Fish

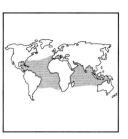

© AMOS NACHOUM / CORBIS

The hammerhead shark is named for its strange-looking head. A thick, flat lobe sticks out on each side of the head. Nobody is sure why the head is shaped like this. The mouth is on the underside of the "hammer." The eyes and nostrils are located at the ends of the lobes. The hammerhead has excellent eyesight and a powerful sense of smell. The skin is very rough. The hammerhead has two fins on the back, the first one much larger than the second.

Like all sharks, great hammerheads swim constantly. Unlike bony fish, sharks do not have swim bladders that let them adjust to water pressure at different depths. If a shark stops swimming, it sinks.

Great hammerheads are found in the open ocean, although they usually remain in shallow waters along coasts and in bays and harbors where the water is calm. They are mainly tropical, but sometimes they swim into cooler waters. As a hammerhead moves along the ocean floor, it swings its head back and forth in search of food. Hammerheads feed mainly on fish, but they will swallow anything they can catch with their razor-sharp teeth. Great hammerheads can be dangerous to human swimmers.

Young hammerheads are born in the summer. Their head is rounder than that of the adult, but its shape changes as the shark grows.

Port Jackson Shark
Heterodontus portusjacksoni

Length: up to 10 feet
Diet: crustaceans
Method of Reproduction: egg
  layer

Home: southwestern Pacific
  Ocean near Australia
Order: Sharks
Family: Horn sharks

 Oceans and Shores

 Fish

© FRED BAVENDAM / PETER ARNOLD, INC.

Many Australians call this relatively harmless shark the "oyster crusher." Rather than biting and slashing, as most sharks do, this species slowly grinds its prey between crushing plates made out of large teeth at the back of its mouth. The Port Jackson shark is also remarkable in that its mouth is placed at the very tip of its snout, rather than beneath it, as with most sharks. Though unusual today, the type of mouth and teeth seen in the Port Jackson shark were common among sharks some 300 million years ago (long before the age of dinosaurs). Species such as the Port Jackson shark are said to be "living fossils," because they are strange survivors from prehistoric times.

When Port Jackson sharks mate, the male bites one of the female's pectoral fins (located just behind her gills) and holds on tight. After the male fertilizes her eggs, the female lays them in tough brown egg cases about 6 inches long. These pear-shaped capsules often wash ashore and are called "mermaid's purses" by beachcombers. In the ocean the leathery eggs may float for as long as five months before hatching. When they emerge, the baby sharks look like miniature versions of their parents.

In addition to oysters and other mollusks, this fish eats most any animal it can find creeping along the ocean floor. Sea urchins seem to be a particular favorite.

Sharksucker
Echeneis naucrates

Length: up to 3 feet
Weight: 15 pounds
Diet: fish and invertebrates
Method of Reproduction: egg layer

Home: warm waters, worldwide
Order: Perchlike fishes
Family: Remoras

 Oceans and Shores

 Fish

© MICHAEL PATRICK O'NEILL / PHOTO RESEARCHERS

What fish would be crazy enough to get close to a shark? Well, there's at least one: the sharksucker. It belongs to a group of fish known as remoras. Countless generations ago, remoras looked like most fish. But over time the fins on the back of their head evolved into suction disks. Remoras use their suckers to attach themselves to bigger fish, on which they ride. Each species of remora has picked out a certain species of fish on which to piggyback. And by its name, you can certainly guess the sharksucker's choice.

The sharksucker has picked a great host. Sharks are fast and have a great sense of smell. This makes them amazingly good hunters. Once the shark has finished with its meal, its little hitchhiker eats the scraps left behind. Sharks don't seem to suffer any harm from their extra baggage. In fact, sharksuckers sometimes clean parasites off their host's back.

Sharksuckers will also attach themselves to various hard objects such as ships and glass bottles. They can be quite difficult to remove. On some tropical islands, clever fishermen have taken advantage of this strength. They put a hook through the sharksucker's tail and drop the fish into the water. When it hits a turtle, the little fish sticks to the shell. Then the fisherman pulls up the sharksucker with the turtle still attached.

Common Shelduck
Tadorna tadorna

Length: about 2 feet
Wingspan: about 4 feet
Weight: 2 to 3 pounds
Diet: fish, fish eggs, insects, algae, snails, clams, and crustaceans

Number of Eggs: about 9
Home: Europe, Asia, and northern Africa
Order: Ducks and screamers
Family: Swans, geese, and ducks

 Fresh Water

 Birds

© ROGER WILMSHURST / BRUCE COLEMAN INC.

Common shelducks are most abundant along Europe's coasts. In Asia, they prefer to live near salty inland lakes and woodland rivers and streams. There's no mistaking this gooselike duck. Its bill is bright red, its feet are pink, and its feathers are boldly patterned.

Compared with other ducks, shelducks spend a considerable amount of time out of water, usually on mud and dry land. They walk and run easily, and even perch on cliff ledges during breeding season. In flight, shelducks look very much like geese, moving with slow and powerful wingbeats.

Most shelducks choose a lifelong mate in the spring of their second year. Together the pair chooses a nest hole. It may be a human-made nest box, a hole in a tree, an abandoned animal burrow, or just a crack in a rocky cliff. The male is a loyal mate, guarding and feeding the female while she sits on their eggs. When they hatch, the ducklings often mingle with neighboring broods.

As ducklings, shelducks bob in and out of the water easily, and often catch small fish and underwater insects. But as the ducks grow plump and fat, they become as buoyant as a cork. Adults float high on the water and have a difficult time ducking beneath the surface. They dive only when extremely frightened.

Crosscut Carpet Shell
Venerupis decussata

Method of Reproduction: egg layer

Home: eastern coastal waters of northern to mid-Atlantic Ocean and Mediterranean Sea

Length: 2 to 3¼ inches

Diet: plankton and dissolved organic matter

Order: Razor clams and their relatives

Family: Venus clams

Oceans and Shores

Other Invertebrates

The crosscut carpet shell is a burrowing clam that lives among rocks in cool and temperate seas. Typically it wedges itself into a rock crevice, anchoring its body in place with its byssus, a tuft of sticky, silky threads. The crosscut belongs to a group of carpet shells called rock venuses. "Rock" refers to where it is found, and "venus" suggests its heartlike shape.

This shell is a bivalve, which means that it has two perfectly matching sides. On the outside, its oval shell is etched with many deep, narrow grooves that cut across the surface in both directions. The surface of the shell is dull to semiglossy and may be white, yellow, or pale brown. The shell's shiny inside surface is white, tinged with shades of orange or purple. Like other carpet shells, the crosscut is quite sturdy. Empty shells often appear on the shore unbroken.

Generally a carpet shell lives anchored in one place for its entire adult life. To feed, it opens the two valves of its shell and allows water to flow over its feathery gills. The gills filter out tiny plankton animals and dissolved bits of plant and animal matter. Like other bivalves, these clams reproduce by spewing their eggs and sperm into the water, where they mix. From the fertilized eggs hatch tiny swimming larvae. The larvae eventually settle on rocks, where they anchor themselves and grow shells.

Common Tree Shrew
Tupaia glis

Length of the Body: 5 to 7½ inches
Length of the Tail: 5½ to 7 inches
Weight: 2 to 6½ ounces
Diet: fruits, insects, lizards, and small mammals

Number of Young: 1 to 4
Home: Southeast Asia
Order: Tree shrews
Family: Tree shrews
Subfamily: Bushy-tailed tree shrews

 Rainforests

 Mammals

© MARK STOUFFER / ANIMALS ANIMALS / EARTH SCENES

The common tree shrew is a very emotional animal. When a male and female meet, it is either love or hate at first sight. The tree shrew's strong feelings become most obvious when two are put into a cage together. About one pair in five seems to fall instantly in love, nuzzling each other day and night. But most of the time, the forced meeting results in a violent fight. Each shrew then retreats as far away from the other as it can. In a cage, however, the couple is forced to look at one another. After a time, they literally die from the stress.

In nature, tree shrews that don't get along can flee. They are very territorial. The male marks the boundaries of his property with scents rubbed from a gland behind his neck. Scents that animals use to communicate in this way are called "pheromones."

A happy tree shrew couple usually mate on the very first day that they meet. About 45 days later, the mother gives birth, usually to two babies that each weigh less than half an ounce. Normally she covers the babies with a special scent, or pheromone, that tells her mate to leave them alone. If she does not, he will undoubtedly eat them.

Tree shrews are more closely related to primates than they are to the molelike shrews of North America and Europe. Like monkeys, tree shrews have large, well-developed brains and apelike ears.

Eurasian Common Shrew
Sorex araneus

Length of the Body: 2¼ to 3⅓ inches
Length of Tail: 1¼ to 2 inches
Weight: ¼ to ½ ounce
Diet: mainly worms and beetles

Number of Young: 3 to 10
Home: Europe and northwestern Asia
Order: Insectivores
Family: Shrews

 Forests and Mountains

 Mammals

© JANE BURTON / BRUCE COLEMAN INC.

Shrews are mouselike creatures that live throughout North America, Europe, and Asia. They can be distinguished from mice by their pointed snout and very tiny ears. In Central Europe the most familiar shrew is the dainty Eurasian common shrew. Like its cousins, this species has long, sensitive whiskers, which are usually in motion. The shrew has very poor eyesight, so it must rely on its whiskers to feel its way in the dark and to find prey.

The Eurasian shrew is common, in large part, because it is able to live in many types of habitat. It is found in forests, scrublands, grasslands, and even partly frozen tundra. The shrew builds "runways" through the leaf litter, grass, and underbrush. It also digs shallow tunnels in the earth and uses the deserted burrows of other animals. Although tiny, this shrew is bold and will fight with animals much larger than itself. It is always hungry and hunts throughout the day and night, pausing only to nap every few hours.

Eurasian common shrews breed throughout the warm months and can give birth to several litters each year. The newborn are naked, blind, and helpless, weighing as little as ¹⁄₁₀₀ of an ounce. They grow quickly and become independent in about one month. The Eurasian species of shrew has several close relatives in North America, including the masked shrew, *S. cinereus*, and the water shrew, *S. palustris*.

29

Eurasian Siskin
Carduelis spinus

Length: about 4½ inches
Weight: about ½ ounce
Diet: mainly seeds
Number of Eggs: 3 to 6

Home: Eurasia
Order: Perching birds
Family: Finches

 Forests and Mountains

 Birds

© HANS REINHARD / BRUCE COLEMAN INC.

The Eurasian siskin seldom stops twittering as it busily searches for seeds among weeds. Its long, rapid song is a series of high, squeaky notes that end with a sustained, wheezy "tsoooeet!" Like its close cousin the canary, the Eurasian siskin's lively chatter makes it a popular cage bird.

The Eurasian siskin is particularly fond of seeds from the prickly carduus thistle (from which this tiny finch gets its genus name, *Carduelis*). Like goldfinches, the siskin has a long, tweezerlike bill, specially designed for extracting tiny seeds from thistles and other seed heads.

The male Eurasian siskin is easily recognized by his black crown and chin patch. The female is grayer than her bright greenish-yellow mate. She has a streaked breast that helps camouflage her in the underbrush. In winter the siskin often feeds with the redpoll, a finch with a bright rosy head. The large, mixed flocks look like colorful confetti dancing over the snow.

The siskin's serenade comes to a frenzied climax in spring. From morning until night, the male siskin serenades the female. As he twitters, the male follows his chosen mate, fluttering his wings with excitement. After breeding, the female builds a cup-shaped nest. The male feeds her for about two weeks as she warms the eggs. Born blind and naked, the chicks need another two weeks before they are ready to fly.

Sand Skink
Scincus scincus

Length: 7 to 8 inches
Method of Reproduction:
  eggs that develop within the
  mother's body

Home: North Africa and Israel
Diet: beetles and other insects
Order: Lizards and snakes
Family: Skinks

 Deserts

Reptiles

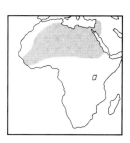

© DANIEL HEUCLIN / PETER ARNOLD, INC.

The sand skink's other name—the sandfish—is perhaps a more appropriate description of its habits. By swinging its body back and forth as it moves across the desert, this skink gives the impression that it is indeed swimming through the sand. Actually, however, it depends on its sturdy legs and long toes to move along.

The sand skink's body is covered with smooth, shiny scales. Its skin is yellow or yellow-brown, with dark crossbands. This coloring helps it blend into its sandy surroundings and conceals it from predators. If it is spotted by a snake or other enemy, however, the skink suddenly disappears by rapidly burrowing into the sand and burying itself.

Early in the morning, when the desert is not quite as hot, sand skinks travel about looking for insects to eat. They may also move around during the middle of the day, when desert temperatures climb to over 100 degrees Fahrenheit; but the skinks cannot let their body temperature rise too high, or they will die. So they often alternate time in the hot sun with time in cooler, shady places or even underground.

The sand skink's eggs develop and hatch inside the female's body. She gives birth to 2 to 10 live baby skinks at a time. A newborn sand skink is only about 1½ inches long, but looks like a miniature adult.

31

Stump-tailed Skink
Tiliqua rugosa

Diet: insects, fruits, earthworms, and snails
Method of Reproduction: live-bearer

Home: Australia
Length: 5 to 12 inches
Order: Lizards and snakes
Family: Skinks

 Deserts

Reptiles

© SUZANNE L & JOSEPH T. COLLINS / PHOTO RESEARCHERS

At first glance, the stump-tailed skink seems to have two heads. This lizard's stubby tail is short and fat, and mimics the shape of the skink's broad skull. This body shape fools predatory birds and other enemies, which often attack the wrong end. When this happens, the stumptail, instead of receiving a killing blow to the neck or head, usually sustains only minor tail damage.

A typical stump-tailed skink has an orange-brown head and back, and is marked with cream-colored blotches and streaks. Its belly is creamy white and flecked with black spots. The skink's scientific species name, *rugosa*, Latin for "wrinkled," refers to the overlapping plates on the creature's head and back. Tough armor helps protect the lizard from the intense desert sun and from attacks by enemies.

This creature lives in Australia's Great Victoria Desert. Active primarily in the early morning, it hides under rocks, sand, or bushes to escape the extreme heat of midday. Stumptails hunt insects among the dry bush and scrub growth. During the brief desert spring, they supplement their diet with blossoming plants and small animals.

Skinks make up one of the world's largest lizard families. They are particularly abundant in Australia and on the surrounding islands in the western Pacific Ocean. The females generally give birth to live young and guard them fiercely.

Hoffmann's Two-toed Sloth
Choloepus hoffmanni

Length of the Body: about 2 feet
Length of the Tail: about 1 inch
Diet: fruits, leaves, and other plant matter

Number of Young: 1
Home: Central America and northern South America
Weight: 10 to 15 pounds
Order: New World edentates
Family: Two-toed sloths

 Rainforests

 Mammals

© TOM BRAKEFIELD / BRUCE COLEMAN INC.

Imagine spending most of your life hanging upside down from the branch of a tree. Imagine eating, sleeping, and talking to your friends in this position. Well, that's how a Hoffmann's two-toed sloth spends most of its time. This slow-moving animal even mates and gives birth while hanging upside down! This seemingly strange behavior actually helps camouflage the sloth. The hair on its legs grows backward, hanging down when the sloth hangs from a branch, much as moss hangs in the rainforest.

The two-toed sloth is active at night, when it depends on its senses of smell and touch to find food. It usually discovers its meals high in the trees but occasionally must descend to the ground to move from one tree to another. This is very dangerous, because the sloth is easy prey for predators.

Jaguars, ocelots, and other cats are the two-toed sloth's main enemies. If a sloth is attacked, it protects itself by lashing out with its two strong front claws and three back claws.

A newborn Hoffmann's two-toed sloth is about 10 inches long and weighs less than a pound. It holds onto its mother's belly with its claws and remains hidden in her fur for several weeks. Then it starts to explore its surroundings part of the day and clings to its mother the rest of the time. By the time it turns nine months, the young sloth is totally independent. The life span of the Hoffmann's two-toed sloth is 30 to 40 years.

Three-toed Sloth
Bradypus tridactylus

Length: 1½ to 2 feet
Length of the Tail: 1 to 3 inches
Diet: tree leaves and buds
Number of Young: 1

Home: northeastern South America
Order: New World edentates
Family: Three-toed sloths

 Rainforests

 Mammals

Imagine a creature that takes hours to travel the length of a single tree branch. Even at its fastest, it may move only about 13 feet a minute. Add to this the fact that this animal's lack of speed actually protects it from predators. Such is the life of the sluggish three-toed sloth. These creatures are so slow that eagles and other predators rarely notice them. Besides, as long as there is enough food within reach, there is no reason for the sloth to move. The sloth depends mostly on touch and smell to find food. Surprisingly, this lazy creature is active both night and day.

The three-toed sloth spends most of its life hanging upside down in trees. It sleeps, eats, mates, and even gives birth in an upside-down position. Its legs are long and slender, with toes that end in strong, curved claws. Its body is covered with a coat of long, rough hair. This hair is home to a variety of living organisms including blue-green algae, which give the brownish coat a greenish color that blends into the surroundings. Several kinds of moths and beetles may also make their home on the sloth's coat!

The three-toed sloth is also called the ai. This name comes from its call, "a-iii," which is commonly heard during the mating season. Females are pregnant for four to six months and must raise the baby with no help from the father. The baby clings tightly to its mother until it is several months old. Then the youngster begins to live on its own. Adult sloths are solitary creatures and do not live in groups.

Red Slug
Arion rufus

Length: about 5 inches
Diet: fungi and decaying matter
Number of Eggs: 18 to 150

Home: Europe
Order: Land snails and slugs
Family: Slugs

 Forests and Mountains

 Other Invertebrates

© TONY WHARTON / FRANK LANE PICTURE AGENCY / CORBIS

The red slug is found in the damp and shady areas of European gardens and woods. A full-time scavenger, it feeds on dung, decaying plants and animals, and fungi such as mushrooms. The slug's mouth is located under the front of its long foot. Inside the mouth are hundreds of tiny teeth arranged in rows on the slug's tongue.

Like most slugs, this species tries to avoid sunlight, which would dry its skin. However, the red slug can tolerate some sun, because it has a built-in sunscreen. This sunscreen, a chemical called porphyrin, give the red slug its vivid color and absorbs some of the sun's burning rays.

The red slug has two sets of tentacles, although only the long second pair are clearly visible. The eyes sit at the tips of the long tentacles. The tiny front tentacles work like a nose, sensing chemicals in the soil and air. With them the red slug can smell a mushroom or other tasty treat up to a foot and a half away.

Slugs are hermaphrodites, which means they are both male and female at the same time. When two red slugs meet, they follow each other, lick one another, and lie close together in a circle. The two slugs then take turns fertilizing each other's eggs. Red slugs lay a few hundred eggs in an entire year, a small number by typical slug standards.

Sand Smelt
Atherina presbyter

Length: up to 6 inches
Diet: small fish, crab larvae, and crustaceans
Method of Reproduction: egg layer

Home: eastern Atlantic coast and the Mediterranean Sea
Order: Silversides and their relatives
Family: Silversides

  Oceans and Shores

Fish

© LAWSON WOOD / CORBIS

Sand smelts are most often seen in midsummer, when they swarm into high shore pools with the rising tide. There they spawn, the females releasing their eggs, and the males fertilizing them. A sand smelt's eggs have many long filaments, or strings, that tangle with each other and with the green algae on wet rocks. In this way the eggs are kept anchored as the tides ebb and flow. When they hatch, newborn sand smelts are just a quarter of an inch long. They stay in their small, warm tidal pools until they grow to at least two inches. At that time the young smelts swim into the sea, where they gather in large schools.

The sand smelt is a vital link in the food chain of the eastern Atlantic seashore.

Predatory fish such as sea bass and birds such as terns and gulls eat huge amounts of sand smelt and depend upon it for their survival. Human beachcombers also catch this small, tasty fish.

The sand smelt is particularly abundant along the North African coast and the Mediterranean Sea. A few venture into the cold waters around Scotland and Denmark. The English named the sand smelt after the true smelt, which it resembles. But the sand smelt belongs to a family of fish known as silversides, a family that includes the grunion and the mullet. In contrast to true smelts, which migrate up streams to spawn, silversides lay their eggs in tidal pools or beach sand.

Giant African Snail
Achatina fulica

Length of the Shell: up to 7 inches

Length of the Body: up to 11 inches

Diet: leaves, flowers, decaying matter, and manure

Method of Reproduction: egg layer

Home: native to Africa; introduced elsewhere

Order: Land snails and slugs

Family: Giant snails

 Cities, Towns, and Farms

 Other Invertebrates

© ROLAND SEITRE / PETER ARNOLD, INC.

The giant African snail is a native of East Africa, but, unfortunately, this pesky creature has found its way to many other parts of the world. It is very adaptable and can live in many kinds of habitats. People have accidentally introduced this species into many places, including Florida. There is evidence that the snails were brought to Florida in the mid-1960s by a young boy returning from a visit to Hawaii. He brought back several of the snails in his pocket. Apparently, he got tired of the snails and let them go. Soon there were thousands of giant African snails in Florida.

A giant African snail can lay hundreds of eggs a year. In a new habitat, the snails multiply rapidly because there are no natural enemies to control the population. They quickly become serious pests that cause a great deal of damage when they feed on garden plants and agricultural crops. In Florida the snails have even chewed paint off houses!

The giant African snail is one of the largest of all snails. It may be as big around as a tennis ball! It has two pairs of tentacles on its head, with its eyes located at the top of the back pair of tentacles. The snail creeps along on its flat foot. Glands in the foot secrete mucus, which lubricates the path over which the creature crawls. If the snail senses danger, it withdraws its head and foot into the protective shell.

African Twig Snake
Thelotornis kirtlandii

Length: 4 to 6 feet
Diet: mainly lizards
Method of Reproduction: egg layer

Home: Central and western Africa
Order: Lizards and snakes
Family: Colubrid snakes

 Rainforests

Reptiles

© TOM MCHUGH / PHOTO RESEARCHERS

The African twig snake is almost impossible to see among the tangled vegetation of the jungle treetops that constitute much of the vegetation in Central and western Africa. Slender as a twig and as long as a vine, this snake wears camouflage spots and dark bars. Its overall color is green, gray, or brown. A band of red extends from the tip of the snake's triangular snout to its neck.

This snake is an extremely fast mover that whips across branches to ambush prey. For the most part, it eats tender lizards, but it also devours the occasional baby bird or small snake. Although the twig snake is active during the day, it has keen vision that allows it to see in the dark shadows of the dense jungle. Its large, bulging eyes enable it to spot small prey several yards away, particularly lizards.

The African twig snake is not aggressive by nature. When disturbed, it prefers to race away rather than to fight. When cornered by an enemy, the snake tries to bluff its way out of danger by inflating its neck and throat and pretending to strike. The snake is able to deliver a deadly bite but seldom does. Its venom is a powerful blood poison, as dangerous to humans as that of its cousin, the dreaded boomslang. Fortunately, the twig snake rarely encounters humans, because it stays in the trees. There the female deposits her eggs in tree holes and in the crooks of large branches.

Corn Snake
Elaphe guttata

Length: 2 to 6 feet
Diet: mainly mice, rats, birds, and bats
Method of Reproduction: egg layer

Home: eastern and central United States and northeastern Mexico
Order: Lizards and snakes
Family: Colubrid snakes

 Forests and Mountains

Reptiles

© JOE MCDONALD / CORBIS

The corn snake is among the most beautiful snakes in North America. This long, slender serpent is named for the black checkered markings on its belly, which resemble the kernel patterns of Indian corn. A corn snake is also distinguished by the arrowhead-shaped marking atop its flattened head. Down the center of its back is a row of large reddish blotches edged in black. Two rows of matching smaller blotches extend along each side. Overall the snake is light orange, brownish yellow, or dark gray.

Corn snakes are most active at night, but often hunt in the early evening. They are agile climbers that can shinny up tree trunks to search through the branches for nestlings and sleeping birds. Corn snakes also climb into the windows and attics of abandoned barns and houses, where they find other food, such as bats and rodents. These snakes are not venomous. To kill their prey, they squeeze and then swallow the suffocated creature whole.

In the wild, corn snakes are most common in lightly planted woods, rocky hillsides, and meadows. Although they don't require a lot of water, they prefer to live near streams and springs. Corn snakes also make their homes in suburban fields and near abandoned buildings. Adults mate from March through early May, and the females lay their eggs from May to July. When the hatchlings emerge in late summer, they are 10 to 15 inches long.

Gopher Snake
Pituophis melanoleucus

Diet: mice, rats, rabbits, pocket gophers, birds and their eggs, and lizards
Method of Reproduction: egg layer

Home: North America
Length: 3 to 9 feet
Order: Lizards and snakes
Family: Colubrid snakes

 Grasslands

 Reptiles

© JOHN SHAW / BRUCE COLEMAN INC.

The gopher snake is not the type of animal people want for a pet—at least, not most people. This big, scary-looking reptile hisses loudly, raises its head, and rapidly shakes its tail when it feels threatened. But it is not poisonous and will not harm people. Actually, the gopher snake is extremely valuable to humans, because it eats many mice and other rodents that destroy crops. It kills these animals by coiling itself around the victim and squeezing—a process called constriction. Then it swallows the prey whole. As you might imagine, digesting such a meal takes quite a long time!

Gopher snakes live in many kinds of habitats, from sandy coastal areas to mountain elevations of 9,000 feet. Grasslands, marshes, forests, and even deserts are home to the reptile. Eastern subspecies are commonly called pine snakes or white gopher snakes; a subspecies that lives in central North America is known as the bull snake. Western subspecies are called gopher snakes. These subspecies all have different color and scale patterns.

In summer, after mating, a female gopher snake lays from 2 to 24 eggs, which are stuck together by a gluelike substance. Each egg is protected by a tough white shell. The eggs hatch in about eight weeks. The young snakes break out of the eggs without any help from their parents. At birth a gopher snake is already 15 to 20 inches long.

Grass Snake
Natrix natrix

Length: 2 to 5½ feet
Diet: mainly frogs; also other amphibians and fish
Method of Reproduction: egg layer

Home: Europe, Asia Minor, and northwest Africa
Order: Lizards and snakes
Family: Colubrid snakes

Fresh Water

Reptiles

© GEORGE MCCARTHY / CORBIS

The grass snake is the gold-medal swimmer of the reptile world. It loves to spend its days in the water, although it also lives in woodlands, on farms, and even in gardens and parks. In the water, it moves by bending its body from side to side, usually holding its head above the water. The grass snake also enjoys lazily floating on the surface of a lake or river. By filling its lungs with air, it can remain underwater for up to 30 minutes.

The grass snake depends on its eyesight for hunting. As soon as it sees a moving frog or other prey, it whips through the water or over ground and catches the victim in its mouth. Then it swallows the prey whole. A grass snake may eat several frogs, one after the other, then not eat again for several weeks. But, despite its excellent hunting instinct, the grass snake has many enemies. Rats and other small mammals eat the eggs and newborn grass snakes. And people kill many adult grass snakes because they fear that these reptiles are poisonous. Fortunately, grass snakes are completely harmless to people.

Most grass snakes hibernate during the cool winter months. They mate in spring, soon after they emerge from hibernation. The female lays her eggs in the middle of summer in hollow logs, under piles of leaves, or in any place that is moist and where rotting plants produce warmth. Depending on her size, the female lays 10 to 40 eggs that hatch in about five weeks.

41

Oriental Beauty Snake

Elaphe taeniura

Length: 5 to 9 feet
Diet: rodents and birds
Method of Reproduction: egg layer

Home: Southeast Asia
Order: Lizards and snakes
Family: Colubrid snakes

 Forests and Mountains

 Reptiles

© DANIEL HEUCLIN / PETER ARNOLD, INC.

Many tropical snakes are greatly feared because they are highly venomous. But the oriental beauty snake is a welcome visitor to the villages and farms of Southeast Asia. It is well liked because it eats rats, mice, and other bothersome rodents. (This snake also eats birds and their eggs.) The oriental beauty snake is completely harmless to people. In fact, it is quite shy and immediately races away when approached. Despite its timidity, this species is seen more often than are most tropical snakes because it is active during the day.

The oriental beauty is named for its handsome cream-colored body and striking dark stripes. A black or dark gray band extends like a mask from the snake's eyes to its neck. On either side of the oriental beauty's body is a lighter, broader band. These "racing stripes" run from the center of the snake's body to the tip of its long, skinny tail. The rear of its body is further decorated with rows of large black blotches that sometimes blend. The snake has a noticeably flat skull, and its neck is distinct from the rest of its body. For a daytime snake, it has unusually large eyes.

Away from civilization, oriental beauty snakes prefer to live along the edges of rainforests and the openings of caves. They catch most of their prey on open ground but prefer to stay near bushes, rocks, and other hiding places.

Red-tailed Pipe Snake
Cylindrophus rufus

Length: up to 3 feet
Diet: mainly small snakes and earthworms
Number of Young: 2 to 12

Home: southeastern Asia
Order: Lizards and snakes
Family: Annelids

  Rainforests

Reptiles

© DANIEL HEUCLIN / PETER ARNOLD, INC.

The red-tailed pipe snake loves to burrow in the squishy mud. Its tunnels often extend three feet or more beneath rice paddies and jungle clearings in Southeast Asia. In this underground maze, the snake hunts smaller snakes and earthworms. Occasionally it surfaces at the edge of a lake or swamp to prey on freshwater eels.

Pipe snakes are primitive serpents. Within their round bodies are the remnants of pelvic bones and hind legs. Such "vestigial" limbs are nature's reminder that all snakes are descended from walking, lizardlike ancestors. Like other pipe snakes, the red-tailed species has small, weak eyes and a round, short head. Its body is covered with flat, shiny purplish-black scales. The end of its tail is also flat, darkly colored on top and bright red underneath.

The pipe snake usually leaves its underground burrow after a heavy rain. If cornered above ground, the snake hides its head under its body while waving the bright underside of its tail. This display often frightens away a wary predator. Pipe snakes are equipped with poison glands. But because of their tooth structure, they cannot inject venom. However, they do bite on occasion.

The female gives birth to live young that measure about seven inches long. Until they are large enough to capture other snakes, the youngsters feed on insect larvae and earthworms.

Tentacled (Fishing) Snake
Erpeton tentaculatum

Length: 16 to 28 inches
Number of Young: 6 to 13
Home: Thailand, Cambodia, and Vietnam

Diet: mainly fish
Order: Lizards and snakes
Family: Colubrid snakes

 Fresh Water

 Reptiles

© SUZANNE L. & JOSEPH T. COLLINS / PHOTO RESEARCHERS

The tentacled, or fishing, snake lives in fresh water, usually in swamps or slow-moving streams. Its most remarkable feature is a pair of movable, fleshy tentacles on its snout. Scientists speculate that the snake wriggles them like lures to attract the fish it feeds on. The feelers may also have chemical sensors that help the snake find prey in muddy water.

Indonesians have a name for this species that translates to "snake like a board." When captured, the reptile stiffens its flattened body and becomes as unbending as wood, remaining motionless even when handled. The tips of its scales are slightly raised, making its skin feel like sandpaper.

This snake is venomous, although not toxic to humans. Two grooved teeth located at the back of its mouth contain venom glands. The venom is toxic to fish, frogs, and other cold-blooded creatures but has little or no effect on warm-blooded animals such as birds and mammals.

The snake's eyes and nostrils are high on its head and directed upward. When the snake surfaces to breathe, only the tip of its snout is visible above the water. While it swims, the snake closes its nostrils with valves that keep out water. The snake spends long periods of time anchored in one place, using its strong, flexible tail to hold onto underwater plants and branches.

Set Index